SELF HEALING WITHIN REACH EVERYONE

3 IN 1. THE ATTRACTION LAW, HO´PONOPONO AND THE HEALING CODE

THREE EASY SELF HEALING TECHNIQUES TO APPLY YOURSELF

CARLOS RIVAS SALAZAR

For you my Angel with all my love ♡

Patricio M.

1

COVER

The three techniques of which we will speak of simple and practical form will help the reader to make by own account simple exercises of self healing. The body has a wonderful system created to heal to the body of natural form it is called immune system.

The first part of the book deals with the love itself, since having a high selfesteem will result in treating or to the physical body, that is to say, the person will eat well and balanced, it will have positive thoughts, it will speak in positive, it will make exercises and in aim all the good one that it serves to maintain mind and body in good state.

Soon the subject of the Law of Attraction is approached, this Law it express that the equal ones are attracted, that is to say, everything in the universe is vibration and the equal vibrations are attracted, for example, if the person is positive and optimistic, it will attract people and positive situations to its life, if on the contrary, she is a negative and pessimistic person, will attract the same thing its life, everything is in the mind, depending on the predominant thoughts that has the person, will emit vibrations to the universe and will attract everything what it is emitted, reason why is necessary to pay attention to the thoughts. We will teach of practical form like using the Law of Attraction in the daily life to attract positive things and to obtain the objectives.

Followed, we will talk of the Ho´ponopono, this technique of sealf healing was developed initially in the towns of Hawaii, Doctor Len it has spread it by the planet, it is a very simple technique that with four words can be healed the memories of past lives or present that affect the people, these four words are: i´m sorry, please forgive me, thank you and I love you. With those simple words we can work painful memories that affect to us in the health, prosperity, love and more.

Finally, a system of self healing is approached received or canalized by the Dr. Alex Loyd, who along with the Dr. Bend Johnson writes on the Healing Codes, these codes help to eliminate stress that cause the ailments or diseases in the physical body, the codes simply eliminate stress allowing the body traverse of the immune system to make the work for which it was programmed that is to cure itself. Of simple form we will explain like being applied the codes himself, with this technique I have seen heal to many people of an endless number of diseases.

In summary, through the Law of Attraction we will learn to think in positive to attract positive things, situations and people to our lives and thus to manage to obtain all the objectives drawn up and to be happy. With the Ho´ponopono we will be able to work the painful memories and negative thoughts that move away us of our goal of being happy and without by some reason after the two previous techniques we have some ailment or disease with the Healing Codes we can treat the stress that caused the ailment or disease to unblock to the immune system and to allow that the body cure itself.

INDEX

Chapter III
Ho´ponopono

Chapter IV
The Healing Codes

PREFACE

It has been always said that a man must seed a tree, have a son and write a book, both first already obtains them, now I am making third, this book I write because I want to spread of a simple form, didactic and direct three wonderful and also very simple self healing techniques.

Many things in the nature are simple, the flowers do not make an effort in growing, simply grow, in the same way, our immune system does not make an effort to maintain to the healthy body, nevertheless, the thoughts and emotions of the people can cause that the body undergoes stress, this stress maintained in the time does that the accumulation of energy somewhere of the body creates a physical annoyance and if continues the situation is transformed into disease.

The three techniques of which we will speak of simple and practical form will help the reader to make simple exercises of self healing.

The first part of the book deals with the love itself, since having a high self-esteem will result in treating well the physical body, that is to say, the person will be fed balanced, it will have positive thoughts, it will speak in positive, it will make exercises and in aim all the good one that it serves to maintain mind and body in good shape.

Soon the subject of the Law of the Attraction is approached, this Law it express that the equal ones are attracted, that is to say, everything in the universe is vibration and the equal vibrations are attracted, for example, if the person is positive and optimistic, it will attract people and positive situations to its life, if on the contrary, she is a negative and pessimistic person, will attract the same to its life, everything is in the mind, depending on the predominant thoughts that the person has, will emit vibrations to the universe and will attract everything what it is emitted, reason why is necessary to pay attention to the thoughts.

Followed, we will talk of the Ho´ponopono, this self healing technique was developed initially in the towns of Hawaii, Doctor Len it has spread it by the planet, it is a very simple technique that with four words can be healed the memories of last lives or the present that the people affect, these four words are: i´m sorry, please forgive me, thank you and I love you. With those words we can work painful memories that affect to us in the health, prosperity, love and more.

Finally, Dr. Alex Loyd received or canalized a self healing codes, Dr. Alex and Dr. Bend Johnson wrote on the Healing Codes, these codes help to eliminate stress that cause the ailments or diseases in the physical body, the codes simply eliminate stress allowing the body through immune system to make the work for which it was programmed that is self healing.

In summary, through the Law of the Attraction we will learn to think about positive to attract positive things, situations and people to our lives and thus to manage to obtain all the objectives drawn up and to manage to be happy. With the Ho´ponopono we will be able to work the painful memories and negative thoughts that move away us of our goal of being happy and without by some reason after the two previous techniques we have some ailment or disease with the Healing Codes we can treat the stress that caused the ailment or disease to unblock to the immune system and to allow that the body only heals.

GRATEFULNESS

I am thankful to God and the Seramitas to give me the inspiration and to send me the thoughts to write this book, to My Mother Nancy del Valle Salazar Cedeño and to My father Jesus Alexander Rivas Oraá to give me to the life and necessary love to develop me like person, to the Fray Luis Amigo School in Venezuela by a good formation, to my wife Belmarelis Lourdes Isnotú Agostino Briceño and to my children Andrés Eduardo, Gabriela Alejandra and Arturo David Rivas Agostino to support to me and to be my source of inspiration.

CHAPTER I
<u>LOVE YOURSELF</u>

WHAT´S MEANS LOVE YOURSELF?

In order to be able to begin this book, we must approach an extremely important subject, since it depends on the love yourself, this writing will arrive at the people or it will happen unnoticed.

In order to be able to advance in the life and any scope we must love to us, this love towards one results in positive things, good health, high self-esteem, excellent disposition to learn new things, to face the adversities of positive form, to have goals in the life, etc.

Unfortunately, in the present society, they bomb to us with words and the negative news, already it seems that the positive being is something strange, the people they see the optimists like dreamers, on the other hand, our parents, professors, relatives and friends with its kindness and limitations, sometimes label us, creating in us mental barriers that costs to surpass, like for example; you are bad, by your fault, you do not serve for the mathematics, you are fat, you are skinny, you are ugly, etc.

All these labels, added to the negative experiences, create barriers, fear, faults, etc to us; that of not surpassing we loaded with them by many years, even by the rest of the life, these memories make difficult love yourself, creating problems of health, love and prosperity.

All these experiences are stored in our conscious mind and subconscious, luckyly we can control our thoughts or to learn to control our mind, is necessary to pay attention to the things that we thought and to the emotions or feelings that we added to them. Remember that you always will have the company of your mind, the 24 hours of the day.

Often the enemy to defeat is you, with your negative thoughts, fear, faults, resentment, wrath, etc. In order to love yourself, we must know clearly our limitations and mental barriers, to confront them and to work on them, when taking conscience from our mental barriers and accepting them, we can work them. The first step then is to become aware, soon to accept them and finally to heal them.

HOW IMPORTANT OUR PARENTS ARE?

In the search of the barriers, we must take into account in the first place our relation with mother and papa, soon with our grandparents, uncles, brothers, etc. From the point of view of the family constellations, each familiar group has an energy, that familiar energy is with her by generations, arriving some times to affect to by 7 generations, for example: in some families it is possible to be observed that the mothers take very badly with the daughters, and is a common denominator who is observed in several generations, or who all the men of the family are divorced, etc.

In such sense, it is important to review the relation with mother and papa, - one of the ten orders says "You honored to your father and your mother" - if some of them were absent, by separation, because it went in a moment with God, if they were, if the relation were bad with some of both, or on the contrary was extremely good, as we know all the ends are bad, for example; if the relation with daughter and papa is extremely good is possible she has been occupied place of mother, this affects the daughter, since unconsciously could be married with papa, reason why the relation with other men could be not possible, due to if she is married with papa is impossible to disappoint the papa love.

These relations with mother and papa can affect the prosperity, love and health. When solving problems with mother and papa, we can honor and love them, so that everything flows, we could be more positive and to obtain all the things that we wished in the life. The therapies of familiar constellations can help to heal the conflicts that can exist with papa or mother, there are many good specialists around the world, being their maximum creative exponent Mr. Bert Hellinger.

HOW TO LOVE OURSELF?

To love ourself means to love our body as it is, to offer good feeding him, to avoid the excesses, vices like the cigarette, alcohol, caffein, to maintain it in form, to feed the positive body and soul with thoughts and feelings, in aim to obtain the happiness. It is necessary to learn to see by one first that to the others, although some people think that is egoism, but if the person is not well with itself, cannot help other people. Everything what we are in our inner world reflects in our surroundings, the life is like an echo, if you do not like what you receive, quick attention to which you emit.

For example, when the fly attendant make the demonstration of how to use the mask, one of the things they clarify is that if the person travels with a child, the mask must be placed first and then help the child, many mothers and parents think, I would put the mask to my child first, but what happens if occur decompression and the person can't breath trying to help child?, both could die, by such reason, you must be well and out of danger, to be able to help to the child. In conclusion, to love yourself is extremely important so that everything in the life flows and manages to have good health, to live with love and to have much prosperity and abundance.

More ahead in this book we will work with three wonderful techniques, of which we found in this universe to solve our circumstances and problems, these tools helped us to focus in the positive things, to erase thoughts or missed beliefs and to heal themselves to we ourself. Let's find them!

CHAPTER II
THE ATTRACTION LAW

WHAT IS THE THE ATTRACTION LAW?

Like any other Law, the law of the attraction acts indifferently of which we know or not as it works. One is which the equal things are attracted, are good or bad. The thoughts are the ones in charge to send the information to the universe, each thing who we thought attracts towards us its equal one, if we have positive thoughts, we will attract positive things, if the negative thoughts predominate, are attracted negative things. What kind of thoughts predominates in your life?

The quantum physics has demonstrated that the molecules that compose all the objects have vibrations, we lived in a vibratory universe, in such sense the thoughts emit vibrations, these vibrations attract the vibrations that are equal, reason why we must have thoughts that are aligned with the things that we want to attract to us.

According to the Law all the people can attract to their lives those goals, objectives, things, health, love and prosperity, knowing well what we wanted, to focus the thoughts and to visualize obtaining what we desired, to have unremovable faith and conviction that we already get. Fear, uncertainty and desperation, incite to have negative emotions, it become in negative vibrations as well, reason why the objective moves away instead of approaching.

HOW FAST DO YOU WANT TO GET YOUR DESIRES?

The quick as the things arrive depends on the feeling that is handled at the time of having the thoughts, while more intense it is the emotion, faster materializes the thing you thought. Imagine a child that wants a toy, his emotion to have the toy is intence, so think like a child. In this point we must mention what the author Louise Hay in her books teaches to us that is to love ourtself and accept us as we are. As we are in our interior is reflected our outer world. It is possible to be affirmed in front of to the mirror every day: "I love and accept my self" Louise Hay

In such sense, it is important to think in positive, visualize your goal and add positive emotions to him. Along with the positive emotions, you have to believe you could get the goal, if you believe and add positive emotions it will become truth. If you think that you can do it or obtain it, you have faith, positive thoughts on which these doing and you add emotions to him or positive feelings the thought thing was materialized. "If you think you can do a thing or think you can't do a thing, you're right." Henry Ford. Take care, equal works of negative form, that is to say, if you have negative emotions and negative, thoughts were materialized and you attract negative things, and as they pass things disagreeable you will attract more of the same and it will become a vicious circle of negative things.

That´s why I recomend, pay attention to the thoughts that you have, if they are negative, change it by positives. Is important to fix attention to things positive to attract the same, is important to focus in abundance to attract abundance, if we paid attention to the shortage we attract shortage, for example, if we focused our thoughts and feelings in the little money that we have, in the low wage that we perceived, we are focusing in the shortage.

WHAT HAPPENS IF WE FOCUSED IN THE SHORTAGE OR THE LACK OF WHICH WE WANT TO REACH?

It is very important to understand and to assimilate this point, usually the people when they have a bad economic situation, for example, always are thinking about that they do not have money, in which the pay does not reach to them after anything, think about the debts and generally they include negative emotions, of rage, frustration, deception, sadness, depression, among others; What doy you think? Exactly! they are focusing in the shortage and the universe gives them more of the same, So that? Because the equal thing is attracted, they are emitting to the universe vibrations of shortage and by its position the universe sends everything what vibrates of similar way. The man of today, is the result of the predominant thoughts of the past. So if you wish to change your present, it must change your thoughts, it forms to act, attitude and feelings in the present, so that you can enjoy a better future.

To my to understand, to manage, to assimilate this point and to become aware from this, constitutes the one of the most important points within this writing, of being understood, reader will manage to reach all the wished one in the life, is concerning the good health, to the love or to the money, because commonest the any human being, is to think and to feel poor, I often listen to say, even comment it with annoyance, as it is possible to think about positive, if I do not have money nor to buy the food, this is the reality, since I make not to think about that, if I am living it. I confess that it is difficult to understand and sometimes costs work to obtain positive thoughts in this type of situations, nevertheless, we must become aware and to understand, that while we focus in the absence of the money, we are focusing to us in the shortage, reason why the universe will give more shortage to us. In those situations we must follow positives, to have faith in God, as they say God tightens but it does not hang, if we have positive attitude and positive thoughts, little by little we will be attracting positive things and we will be able to leave that situation.

HOW I FOCUS IN WHICH I WANT?

We must fix our attention to which we want to obtain or to have, if i want a monthly salary of $ 8,000, for example, I am focusing and visualizing what I want, no matter if it not true in my present, when i thinking about which i want, i attract that i wished. The universe will be in charge to fix all the things so that we obtained that we thought.

If you want something material, for example a car, you must see the car that you want, if it is possible to go to selling cars and to rise in, to take a photo within the car to be able to see it every day, to go to the bank to ask the requirements for the loan, etc, in aim to visualize what you wanted, to have faith in that you will reached, finally, when the car arrives, to celebrate and to thank to the divinity.

HOW ATTRACT A LOVE TO OUR LIVES?

The Law works in the same way for all the things, if you wish a couple love in your life, you must focus in which you want, that is to say, you can write a letter with sex of your love, age, qualities that you want, fisical complex, loving gay, good mood, in short, all the things which you wish to attract to your life, you can make a the treasure map, to put a photo of a beautiful person, who you want to attract, with positive faith, patience and thoughts, the person will arrive. Usually what happens, people are hopeless, put themselves to look for from the shortage, the lack of love, complain to be single, that nobody wants them, etc, by their position, attract more solitude. It is possible to mention that besides to make all these things, we must be well with ourself and love us and as we are, if we considered ourselves ugly, boring, fat, by all means that the person never will arrive, because when we have low self-esteem and those negative thoughts of ourself, the universe will attract people who will say that you are ugly, fat, boring, etc, since that is what you think of yourself, so the first step is to love yourself, when you loves yourself other people will love you as you are and will value you as a person.

If you only pay attention to the physicist, it is attracting from the vanity and the ego, and that type of relations lasts little, since the physical body is deteriorated with happening of the years, when you are looking for real love, will attract people who value it and they love you by how you are, those relations can last all the life.

HOW CAN MAINTAIN OR ATTRACT GOOD HEALTH TO OUR LIVES?

The good health is a normal condition for the human being, and in general it is true, unfortunately, the mass media focus in the diseases, the statistics always reflect the amount of people with one or another disease. They focus in the disease and they cause that the people focus in the diseases, create fear and panic in the people.

If by circumstances of the life, some disease is had, instead of focusing in the disease, to speak with everybody about it, to assume victim role, it is due to let think about the disease. You must visualize you healthy, cured, positive attitude, see humorous films, laugh, in order to attract positive things and heal. You always must focus in which you wanted, in the final result, in this case is health, to be healthy. Repeat every day, I am healthy, thank for the good health.

We must create good and positive habits, By all means that also we must be fed well, try to eradicate the red meats, as always Doctors recommend, eat vegetables and fresh fruits, include dry fruits such as peanut, almonds, etc, drink abundant water, eat carbohydrates one or maximum twice a day, eat low in salt and sugar refined, aim a good one and balanced feeding, and do exercise. This together with the positive thoughts will attract a good health.

TAKE CARE OF HOW DO YOU THINK AND SPEAK

Going deep a little in positive thought and taking some points from Neuro-Linguistic Programming (NLP), we must learn how to speak in positive, that is to say, due to lessons that we received from diverse sources the words <u>NO</u>, <u>NOT</u>, <u>DON´T</u> is in our everyday language, for example, if we want to go to a place and arrive fast, we thought, I hope there is No traffic, if we go to the bank, I wish there are Not meny people at the bank, I wish there is not rain, I do Not want to smoke, etc.

The problem is that the brain works with images, when somebody says the elephant, automatically the brain imagines an elephant, like a picture, in such sense, the words are transform into images, nevertheless the word NO, is impossible for the brain to turn the world NO into image, if we thought or we say I do not want to smoke, the brain eliminates the word NOT (since it cannot make graphic) and the barin imagines the person smoking, reason why really will attract continue smoking. The idea would be to say I am going to quit smoke.

Other examples, I hope there is little people in the bank, I want to arrive early, to the children, instead of saying to them do not run, is possible to be replaced by walking please, instead of do not touch that, you can say, leaves it, etc. At the beginning could be difficult to speak in positive, the first step is to become aware, that is to say, whenever we think about negative, to realize our word and to try to create the phrase in positive.

EVERYTHING REMAINS IN THOUGHT OR IT IS DUE TO ACT?

Of course there is important to think before act, but without action there is no reaction, we must work to get what we want, if we want to gain the lottery, we must buy a ticket first to have the option to win. If we want a new job, we must send the curriculum to several sites to have options. God Said: help yorself that I will help you. We also mentioned the concept of madness of Albert Einstein: "To do always the same and to wait for different results". All thought must go accompanied of an action and all action creates a reaction, is important not only to dream and to visualize what it is wanted, since without action everything will remain in dreams and we will become in dreamers, is necessary to act and to make that the things happen, work for the profit of the objectives. We can create a plan, with its defined steps, times to reach the objectives finally to obtain the drawn up goal. While more specific we formulate the plan, more probabilities of obtaining the objectives and finally the goal we will have. Let´s work!

WHAT DO I DO WHEN OBTAIN THE GOALS?

Finally to be thankful, when solicited thing is received, thank the divinity and the universe for the obtained thing. Even before receiving, we can thank for all the good things that we have, good health, beautiful family, a car, job, etc, be thankful helped us to focus in the positive things of the life and attract more positive things and persons.

Also the profits are due to celebrate, in this form we sent a message to the gratefulness to the universe, on the other hand, we give us a permission to enjoy the success, well deserved after the effort. We can observe the celebrations in the baseball equipment, whenever a player makes a good play or hit a home run, all the equipment leaves to receive to the player like a hero.

WHAT WE PROPOSE TO OBTAIN THE OBJECTIVES?

1. - To identify the objective goal or what is wanted to reach: It is important to be clear what you wanted, if you want a new car, for example, you must describe the car, color, model, motor, brand new or used car and very important to specify when you want to get the car, that´s means the time (in a year, in three month, etc), someday I want to have that car, is something unattainable, since someday it does not exist, is not possible to be measured.   Also it is important to look for goals that can be reached to avoid the doubts and frustration. We can be looking for goals a little smaller and go up in our aspirations. Please remember to think the goal in positive, avoid use the word "NOT", affirmations can be used that begin with: I am in process of… I am on way to… The goals, well specific must be written, with all possible details and to review them every two months, you can make a map of the treasure to visualize the goals.

2. - To focus in the goal: Think about positive on the goal, how to obtaining it, all the steps to follow to obtain it. Add positive emotions on which it is

wanted, visualize obtaining the goal, see yourselve within the car, handling it, with possitve emotions.

3. - To cause that the things happen, draw up a plan of how obtaining the objective, moving, work to obtain the wished thing.

4. - Thank for all good things you already had before obtaining the things, this aid to focus us in positive and for being with good attitude. After obtaining the goals, thanking to the divinity and to the universe. We can make a similarity of the profit of the objectives with a person who harvests fruits: This person clean first the land and works it, that is to say, it is necessary to release of negative thoughts our mind, to think the positive, to create the habit of the positive thought.

Soon it plants the seed of the fruit that it wants to harvest, in our mind seeds the seed of which it is wanted to obtain with the greater possible details, either specific, that is to say, to have clear intention, know the goals, put to him positive emotions to obtain the objectives with greater speed.

Next the person comes to clear the weeds of the land, reason why it is important to have faith, to eradicate the fear that moves away to us of the goal, remember that the fear is to focus in the absence of which is wanted or to have doubts to obtain the goal, this moves away to us of the objective.

Finally, act, formulate the plans for the profit of the objectives and to cause that the things happen.

In Summary:

The thoughts become things, everything what we thought is positive or negative is materialized in our world. All the material things have vibration, even the money, if our thoughts vibrate in syntony with which we want, vibrations are attracted.

Mateo 7 says:

Request, and will occur them;

Look for and you will find;

Call and it will be opened to you

Because all the one that requests, receives;

The one that it looks for, finds:

And the one that calls, is opened to him

When we added positive emotions to the things, they are materialized more quickly. For example, when we want new a cellular one, we imagined it, we see it in the store and we were touched when seeing it, that positive emotion attracts that new cellular one and it is materialized. In order to have emotions we must be well with us, to love ourself.

We must focus in which we want to obtain it, in the abundance, if we paid attention to the lack of which we want or in the shortage of money for example, we will attract more shortage. Only think about which we want. The brain works with images, the word "NO" is impossible to imagine, reason why when we thought about not taking alcohol, the brain imagines to the person drinking and it is attracted more of the same.

Act, work for things you want to get, be specific, if you want a new job, you must look for it. Finally, thank for the obtained thing, thank to the divinity and to the universe.

CHAPTER III
HO'OPONOPONO

WHAT IS THE HO´PONOPONO?

Ho´oponopono is a very old Hawaiana technique of healing and it is defined as "mental cleaning", at the modern time the Kahuna or Master Morrnah Nalamaku Simeone create the Ho´oponopono self Identity, its lessons were happened to the Dr. Ihaleakala Hew Len, the Dr. Len dictates seminaries anywhere in the world spreading this wonderful and simple technique of cleaning of the memories that can affect to us in our daily life.

In order to understand the technique we must have an ample and open mind to accept that we are spiritual beings in a physical body, that our soul comes traveling and reincarnated many lives to obtain the necessary learnings for the spiritual growth of the soul. In that order of ideas, the memories of each life are stored in the akashic records, to understand this in our modern world, we could say that it is a hard disk that stores our memories of past lives and present, these archives are interlaces with our subconscious mind.

HOW AFFECTS THESE MEMORIES TO US?

These memories generally try to protect us of damages suffered in past lives or the present one, trying to maintain us alert and to avoid to suffer similar damages to which is in our memories. Nevertheless, sometimes these memories, can obstruct our life, because fear can cause us to make certain things, to obtain objectives, creating fear treating "to protect us".

These fears can paralyze to us and avoid that we advance in the life. These fears can go from fear to take in an elevator, fear to make activities, to make important businesses to fear to have money. It says that the life is like a mirror, everything that is in our reality is a reflection of our inner world, all people are in our life to show us something that we must heal within ourself, if someone criticizes to another one, means that we must heal the critic, if bothers me the negative attitude on a person, we must heal negative in us, Dr. Len says that all those things are memories that are in us and we must heal them by means of the technique of ho´oponopono.

In such sense, Dr. Len speaks of being responsible for all the things that are in our life, since if appears in our reality it is because they are memories that are showing something to us that we must heal in our interior, no matter how bad the situation are, when doing us responsible, we can work on us to resolve the situation, never the solution to the problems this outside, always this within us, working with the technique and healing, the situation will change to us and everything will improve.

WHAT IT DEALS WITH THE TECHNIQUE?

When we apply technique we requested to divinity, that through universal and unconditional love cleans and purifies the origin of these problems, these are the memories. These memories can be own, inherited or simply of the group of the humanity. With respect to the last point, the group of the humanity or collective subconscious mind, we can say that many religious beliefs exist that they label to us as sinners, these "sins" are within the mind of the humanity, good or bad, these memories sometimes affect to us or they inhibit us to make certain things.

It is possible to emphasize that ho´ponopono part from the point that all the human beings are united, by this collective mind and what it affects one affects all and also it is certain that what heals to each person with the technique we are healing it all in the planet, this is the wonderful thing of this healing technique.

It is phrase that we could call header (we will give examples of these phrases more advanced) and the four always used words, these words are: i´m sorry, please forgive me, thank you and I love you.

Let´s Explain a little the four key words, if we assumed the responsibility of all the things that affect to us, in the health, love and economy, says I´m sorry by the situation that is happening and that it affects to us, accepting our responsibility, we requested pardon, please forgive me, we thank to the universe for teach us what we must heal and finally we added the used word to express the purest and powerful energy, on which is based all the universe and the divinity that is the love (I love you). i´m sorry, please forgive me, thank you and I love you. It is that simple, to accept responsibility of things that happens to us, since everything what happens in our lives we must heal it from our interior, to say i´m sorry reason why it happens, no matter how much it can cost to us to request forgiveness, to thank the divinity to allow us to heal the memories and finally to say the word that all cures, I love you. The technique of Ho´oponopono is very simple, sinple to say some phrases to clean the memories and to loosen those thoughts.

Then "i´m sorry" and "Please forgive me". You say this to acknowledge that something (without you knowing what it is) has gotten into your body/mind system. You have no idea how it got there. You don´t need to know. If you are overweight for example, you simply caught the program that is making you that way. By saying i´m sorry, you are telling the Divine that you want forgiveness inside you, you are asking de Divine to help you forgive yourself.

From there you say "thank you" and "I love you". When you say "tank you", you are espressing gratitude. You are showing your faith that the issue will be resolved for the hihest good of all concernd. The "I love you" transmutes the energy form stuck to flowing. It reconnects you to the Divine.

HOW TO USE OF PRACTICAL FORM THE HO´PONOPONO?

Let´s see the most common phrases that we can use:

Divinity, heals within me the painful memories and the mistaken beliefs that they can cause this economic shortage, i´m sorry, please forgive me, thank you and I love you (repeat the four words as many times as you want, there is no rule of the number of repetitions).

Divinity, heals within me the painful memories and the mistaken beliefs that they can cause this one rage that I feel towards this person, i´m sorry, please forgive me, thank you and I love you. Remember that if I feel rage of any actitud of a person, that´s means this emotion is inside of me, so that we must work to heal it.

Divinity, heals within me the painful memories and the mistaken beliefs that can cause this fear to travel in airplane, i´m sorry, please forgive me, thank you and I love you.

Divinity, heals within me the painful memories and the mistaken beliefs that can cause this disease in me, i´m sorry, please forgive me, thank you and I love you.

Please forgive me by what is within me that contributing to get this situation in my life. i´m sorry, please forgive me, thank you and I love you.

Divinity please cleans and transmutes all the errors of thought that is pronounced in my life like beliefs that the money is bad, dirty, etc. i´m sorry, please forgive me, thank you and I love you.

Divinity, heals within me the painful memories and the mistaken beliefs that can cause some disadvantage to me in this wonderful day, i´m sorry, please forgive me, thank you and I love you. (This phrase can be used all the mornings before leaving home).

Divine creator, father, mother, son as one, if I, my family, relatives and ancestors, have offended you, your family, relatives and ancestors in thoughts, words, deeds and actions, from the beginning of ur the creation to the present, we ask your forgiveness…Let this cleanse, purify, release cut all the negative memories, blocks, energies and negative vibrations and transmute these unwanted energies to pure light…And it is done.

i´m sorry, please forgive me, thank you and I love you. (you can say this phrase when you feel a person without any reason has rage, bothers to us, or we to her).

To your body: I love you the way you are. If I have abused you in any way, I ask for your forgiveness. Thank you for the breath of life and the beating of our heart.

I release to all those of those who I believed to receive damage, because they give me back formerly what I did to them before in another life: i´m sorry, please forgive me, thank you and I love you. (As we commented at beginning, many memories come from passed lives, generally when somebody makes something negative, means that we are paying some Karma of another life, simply is the Law of the Karma, the Law of the Compensation, all the bad things that we do we must pay it, this karma must be paid in this life or in another one, but everything is not bad, also can be created Darmas, that is positive things)

By that so difficult relation from which I keep so many bad memories: i´m sorry, please forgive me, thank you and I love you.

If my physical body experiences anxiety, preoccupation, blames, fear, sadness or pain I say: memories "I LOVE YOU", I am been thankful to have the opportunity to release them to you and to me: i´m sorry, please forgive me, thank you and I love you.

I declare myself peacefully with all the Earth people, and with who I have pending debts: i´m sorry, please forgive me, thank you and I love you. (It is a generic form to clean)

Heavenly Father, I ask for the protection of your great white light around my physical body and mental arena. I thank you that each day you send your angels to accompany me everywhere I go keeping me safe and protected in every way. And it is so.

You can also insert the name of friend or loved one in this prayer

Make this your mantra. Say during commercials on TV, in the car, waiting in line at the store, at the doctor´s office, anytime anywhere. Silently or aloud.

Say these four phrases as often as possible, either aloud or silently.....especially when you are feeling negative feelings about anything or anyone..... Say the prayer about all that comes into your experience. If you hear or see anything that evokes emotion, or negative feelings, use the prayer.

Is very important to say the phrases without any expectation, to say them to the divinity with faith and only trust that the painful memories are being cleaned. In conclusion with these simple words and phrases we will clean the memories that create the conflicts, the Dr. Len has healed too many people with this simple method and for me use every day and I give faith it of which it works.

CHAPTER IV
THE HEALING CODES

HOW BEGAN EVERYTHING?

Some years ago, specifically in 2001, Alex Loyd was in the search of some medicine that cured to its wife of a great depression, had crossed the best specialists of the traditional medicine, without obtaining good results, he continued its search in the alternative medicine, a day when he traveled from return to its house in airplane, he had received or canalized some codes, at the outset didn´t know what he received, didn´t even know if he had received some information or if he was becoming crazy.

Accepting with love the received thing, he began to prove it with his wife and little by little it was improving, soon trusted the technique to some close friends, the results were positive, until a day a person who had suffered a serious disease made the curativos codes during months and surprising he cure herself completely of the disease.

In that point Loyd became aware from which these codes could cure almost any disease, at this days Loyd dictates seminaries everywhere. Alex Loyd along with Ben Johnson, wrote the Healing Codes book, of this book we extract the mentioned information and we summarized it for facility of the reader.

HAS THE TECHNIQUE SOME SCIENTIFIC BASEMENT?

The technical has been proven scientifically with numerous tests that validate from the point of view of the traditional medicine, that it obtains excellent results in more of a 90% of the studied cases. Dr. Loyd only after have verified scientifically that the codes work, began to disclose the information. Scientifically speaking, 95% of the diseases are generated by mental stress and/or corporal, that is to say, any type of stress creates a imbalance to us, this stress is transformed into discomfort and the discomfort becomes illness.

MUST WE FEAR TO THE ILLNESS?

The disconfort and the illness are our friends, thanks to them our body indicates that something is wrong and that we must pay attention, the human body is like the board of a car, when the red light of the water turn on, warns that we must throw water to the car, otherwise the motor will break down. Of the same form the discomfort and soon the illness warns to us that we must be reviewed and resolve the situation to cure to us.

The body has by nature the innate capacity to healing itself. The Dr. Loyd discovered that stress inhibits the faculty of the body to cure itself, the healing codes cleans stress and allows that the immune system of the body is reestablished to the 100%, of that form, without concerning the disease the healthy body. Reason why the healing codes do not heal the disease, simply eliminate stress that causes the inhibition of the immune system, soon the body makes their work.

WHAT STRESS CAUSE TO THE HUMAN BODY?

Stress attacks the central nervous system, creating an imbalance in the hypothalamus and the hypophisis, these due to stress secretes hormones in the sanguineous torrent looking for to resolve the stress situation. Of not being solved the situation a malaise is created, this can be anywhere of the body, usually in the weakest point of our body. Usually all the people have a heel of Aquilles, that is to say, everyone have a weak point, some get dizzy in a boat, that is to say, that its weakness is the stomach, others suffer of headaches, some feel pains in the kidneys, or it costs to them to breathe, in short, all we have a weak point and possibly it is there where stress is accumulated. The Dr. Loyd explains (and in this point it agrees with the Law of the attraction and ho´oponopono), that when the heart and the conscious mind are in conflict, the heart wins, in this case the heart is denominated to the subconscious mind.

We are going to explain a little bit, had said in the part of the Ho´oponopono that we had memories of past and the present lives, those memories store in the subconscious mind, these usually try to protect of some damage, when a conflict between the subconscious mind and the conscious one exists, the subconscious desire to us, for example, if when young we remained locked up in an elevator and we entered panic and we thought then that we were going to die, of adults, when we enter an elevator, the fear memory activates, and although consciously i know that it is not going to happen nothing to me, the subconscious desire and activates the fear to avoid that it happens to me something in the elevator. These

35

memories cause stress and can trigger later in a malaise and in disease. The curativos codes work on that memory eliminating the stress situation, really do not eliminate the memory, they only change to the perception eliminating the fear and therefore disappearing stress.

If we spoke of passed lives, once a person had panic to the water of sea, is that in a last life she had suffocated, by such reason was created that panic and stress, as we commented these memories are stored in the subconscious mind, the curativos codes help to eliminate this stress. If you want to go deep in the subject of passed lives, you should read books of Bryan Weiss, are excellent.

HOW HEALING CODES WORKS?

These codes work with the universal energy, our body canalizes the energy through the ends of the fingers, these serve like antennas that emit energy, this energy flows by our fingers and it is applied in four specific points to eliminate stress.

Although it seems something esoteric, as this technique commented at the outset has passed all scientific test verifying that in a 90% it cures to the patients.

On the other hand, the scientific community has accepted and demostrated, that we are energy and that in our body there is sufficient energy to illuminate to a whole city.

WHICH ARE THE FOUR POINTS?

1. - The Bridge: This is in the final part of the partition of the nose, where it would be the union of the eyebrows. The codes works the pituitary gland (frequently one talks about to him like the masterful gland because it controls the main endocrine processes of the organism) and the pineal gland.

2. - The Adam's apple: It works the spinal marrow and the central nervous system, in addition to the thyroid.

3. - The Jaw: It works on the reactive emotional brain, including the tonsil and the seahorse, in addition to the spinal marrow and the central nervous system.

4. - The Temple: The superior functions of the right and left brain and the hypothalamus.

In other words, the control centers treat for each system, each organ, and each cell of the organism. The curativa energy of all these centers flows towards all of them.

HOW AND WHERE CAN BE DONE THE CODES?

Take a look for a calm place, relax, takes several deep breathings and you do the following sequence:

1. – Qualify the subject you are going to work from 0 to 10, being the zero minimum and 10 most painful.

2. - Identifies the nonhealthful feelings and/or beliefs that they are related to this subject.

3. - Look for memories: It thinks about retrospective if there were some other moment in your life when you have felt in the same way, even if the circumstances had been different. We are looking for same type of feelings or sensations. Take the earliest memory that emerges, and focus in curing that first.

4. – Qualify your memory from 0 to 10, could have more than one, works the first most painful one.

5. - Repeat the oration with initial subject you want to work with and the found memories.

"I pray that you would find, open, and heal all known and hidden negative images, beliefs, cellular and generational memories, and all resulting physical issues, related to [insert the issue, e.g. "any unforgiveness issues that are at the source of his/her issue"], by filling [your name] with the love, life, and light of the Most High God. I also pray that you would magnify the effectiveness of this healing to the maximum level for [your name] highest good, at an optimal pace, and restore everything to your original design. Thank you, God."

6. - Holding each position by about 30 seconds, mantain a small distance between your hands and the body without sticking the hands to the body, repeats the four positions at least three times. Also you can do ho´oponopono mentally to the situation while beams the positions, you can think about positive things or maintain the mind in target like in a meditation. This exercise can last about 6 minutes or the time that you decide.

7. - After finishing the exercise, take a look to your initial subject again and the memories, must have lowered. If lack, you even can make the procedure again, until you feel that the worked memories is not a problem for you or who does not create any negative feeling in you.

You can do the healing codes once a day, can be in the early morning or at night before sleeping, if the situation is complex, you could do it two or three times a day, until you feel that the problem has disappeared, if is a disease you can do two or three times a day by a time until the disease disappears.

One of my patient who by many years showed in the seborrhea skin, that is to say, white wheals in many parts of the body, she began twice a day with the codes, every day during three weeks and when we met, almost all wheals disappeared and the pink skin was seen, was very exciting to see it.

CAN BE APPLIED THE CODES FOR OTHER PEOPLE?

You can make the healing code for another remote person or pet, you follow the same procedure and add the name of the person or animal:

"I pray that you would find, open, and heal all known and hidden negative images, beliefs, cellular and generational memories, and all resulting physical issues, related to [insert the issue, e.g. "any unforgiveness issues that are at the source of his/her issue"], by filling [person's or animal´s name] with the love, life, and light of the Most High God. I also pray that you would magnify the effectiveness of this healing to the maximum level for [person's or animal´s name] highest good, at an optimal pace, and restore everything to your original design. Thank you, God."

WHAT OTHER THINGS CAN WE WORK?

Also we can work twelve points if we don´t have some specific problem, with these twelve points we work the body in general and the most important systems, the words of each point should be add to the main oration after "all resulting physical issues, related to":

1. - Lack of pardon: Rage, wrath and fear

2. - Harmful Actions: Love yourself, self-esteem, self-destruction, self-sabotage.

3. - Mistaken Beliefs: Missed beliefs on my self, my life, self-esteem.

4. - Love versus Egoismo (endocrine system or hormonal/glandular system): Love to my self, love for my relatives, love by the life, egoism.

5. - Joy versus Sadness/Depression (the skin): Sadness, depression, to enjoy the life, love to the life.

6. - Peace versus Anxiety/Fear (the gastrointestinal apparatus): Fear, sadness, impatience, difficulty to trust others, inner peace.

7. - Patience versus Wrath/frustration/impatience (immune system): Wrath, comparison, frustration, displeasure, impatience.

8. - Amiability versus Rejection/Severity (central nervous system): Egoism, rejection, severity.

9. - Kindness versus Not to be sufficiently good   (respiratory system): Fault, shame, fear, not to believed good.

10. - Confidence versus Control (reproductive system): Control and confidence.

11. - Humility versus image control (the circulatory system): Vanity and lack of humility.

12. - Automatic control versus to be outside control (the muscle-skeletal apparatus): Lack of control and wrath.

HOW TO RECOGNIZE IF WE MUST WORK EACH ONE OF THESE POINTS?

1. - Lack of pardon: You can recognize it when the person shows Wrath or irritability, rages, fear or don´t wanting to be near a person. Many people who are conscious of their lack of pardon do not want to let it go because they feel that they would be like letting flee to the author of his crime.

2. - Harmful Actions: When the heart or subconscious mind and the head enter conflict, the heart is the one that wins. The harmful actions come given by thoughts like: I am not the sufficiently good, people will do damage to me, my life does not have remedy, I cannot trust anybody, all are better than I, it cannot do that. Harmful actions like excess of food, alcohol, cigarette, drugs, excess of medicines, excess of work, all the fact in excess that it damages to the physical body.

3. - Mistaken Beliefs: What it sickens us in 100% of the times it is the stress that is caused when having a belief mistaken about ourself, of our lives, or other people. These beliefs cause that we are scared when we would not have to be it, stress and suffering are simply the fear that has been gotten to present/display of physical form. These beliefs are the tumors contained within our cellular memories that propagate the disease and the sufferings of our lives. We always do those that we create. And everything what we do, we do it due to something in which we create. If your beliefs are correct, your feelings, thoughts and conducts will be healthful. If you are doing, thinking, or feeling something that you do not want, he is always due to that you create. If you change your beliefs, your thoughts and your actions everything will change automatically.

4. - Love versus Egoism: Love is the virtue from which all the other virtues emanate. The true love, is to forget to me, my own necessities and desires until the point to do what is better for other people and to me. If the election is between my own necessity or desire and another person well, the love will choose the other person.

On the other hand, a lack of love is the root of virtually all the problems that we have. The apparatus or system of the body for the category of love, is glandular endocrine or hormonal system. As all the other virtues emanate of the love, and all the negative things emanate of the egoism, therefore the endocrine system is a vital part of all disease or well-known suffering.

The low self-esteem tends to be in the form of hormonal problems and glands. To make the healing codes on this category will cure the problems of love, egoism and endocrine.

5. - Joy versus Sadness/Depression: The presence or absence of true joy is a very good indicator of where is the person in her conscious mind. The joy is one of the first things that are lost when the nonphysical or physical problems, are pronounced. The true joy blooms in the Earth of the love. In where there is love, there is joy. A love absence will be correlated with a joy deficiency, always.

The corporal system related to the category of the joy is the skin (the integumentary system), which is the greatest organ of the body. Usually depressed people have some kind of skin problem. Sadness and depression have their origin in the cellular memories, whose lie is that the life does not have remedy by which happened in the past.

6. - Peace versus Anxiety/Fear: Peace is the best indicator of the health of heart. Why? This is the unique one of the virtues in which you cannot work to create more of her through effort. It is the natural result of a loving heart. Peace is disturbed by the fear, and the fear is the father of all the negative feelings. Sadness, impatience, difficulty to trust others, bad behaviors, self-indulgence, all originate by the fear. The fear is a reaction before a pain. Although all experience pain, some choose the love and others choose the fear. Remember, when the head and the heart enter conflict, the heart is the one that wins. Even if your conscious and rational election is the love, the fear wins and it robs your peace to you. If you have a negative emotion, were brought by the fear, if you have some physical malaise, it came through corporal apparatus of the category of Peace, the gastrointestinal apparatus. Almost each disease and suffering is originated somehow through gastrointestinal apparatus.

7. - Patience versus Wrath/frustration/impatience: The impatience is the evidence of which we are not satisfied or contentments. Comparing us to ourself leads to us to superiority or inferiority feelings. This feelings cause stress and health problems. If you have feelings of irritability, frustration, wrath or of insecurity, you must work on it. The evidence of the nature pivot of this one category is in the immune system. We found that the immune system is disconnected by the wrath and its many affiliated, and by a nonhealthful belief that something must change in order to be good. Amazingly, when the cellular memories concerning the wrath, comparison, and the displeasure are solved, the physical sufferings tend to cure themselves of dramatic way. This happens by means of returning to ignite the immune system.

Each feeling and negative emotion, including impatience and wrath, originally come from fear. The wrath seems to be the indicator that the fear has gone far enough in the life of somebody like disconnecting the immune system. You cannot solve the problems of wrath without also treating the fear. One has noticed that when it works patience and wrath, the immune system returns to connect itself.

8. - Amiability versus Rejection/Severity: An egoistic person (one who reacts by fear, instead of choosing love) is probable that rejects and that is severe or lasts with other people, because its own pain and its own feelings by ricochet. This is most devastating than somebody can feel in the life (the rejection of another person).

It is in the root of almost any problem of love (to feel accepted, loved and feeling that it is worth the trouble). The system of the body that is affected more by the rejection is the central nervous system. The central nervous system would have to be considered the control mechanism for almost any other function. The million signals that coordinate the activities and movements of the conscious and unconscious body are controlled by the central nervous system. Two of the most important parts are the spinal marrow and the brain. This makes stress the gravity of the rejection when we understand that the system more damaged by this rejection is the main system of control of the organism. The things that more directly cure to the central nervous system, are the simple acts of amiability.

9. - Kindness versus Not to be the sufficiently good: Several people have the category of kindness like their main problematic category, specially the people who have undergone emotional abuse, perfectionism, or legalist or fundamentalist religion. Fault, shame and fear are enormous subjects here. A huge group of people whose subjects are in this category are perfectionists. This it is a difficult subject, since many people who really fight with the perfectionism think that that is a good and admirable quality, similar of certain form to be addict to the work. The addict ones to work frequently is praised by their hard work, so it can be difficult to see that it really is little healthful. To the power not to be perfect, the people depress themselves, suffer of hopelessness and amazingly they think that they are bad. The system of the body for this category of kindness is the respiratory system. When somebody is scared, it blames and shame, the physical reaction commonest is the difficulty to breathe.

10. - Confidence versus Control: It is not possible to be loved without trusting. Without confidence, always we have an egoistic barrier of protection that inhibits love. Or in relations, health, profession, the extreme control leads generally to health problems. The control leads to the wrath, frustration, misunderstood, and in the end to distrust, and not to the love

nor to the privacy. This this related to the reproductive system. The loving privacy runs with the fuel of the confidence. If you take the confidence, everything what you have is sex without privacy.

11. - Humility versus The control of the image: The image is it everything, that is at least what the advertising campaigns sell to us. The control of the image is originated in a belief that I must be well physically whatever it cost, I need that people see me beauty instead of see who I really am. The problem comes when this makes us put our energy in which it is not a real image. The circulatory system is the affected one with this conflict.

12. - Self control versus to be out of control: If we don´t have self control, we cannot love, we cannot make our dreams, and we would end quickly our health generally. If our heart is with fear, then we must have the control of which it is required in order to be well. The muscle-skeletal apparatus is the one that is affected more directly by the self control subjects. He has been amazing having information of clients who report that the muscle-skeletal problems were cured after the subjects of the heart of the laziness cured, feeling with right, hopelessness, rectitude, etc.

These twelve points can be worked separately, a point per day or a point by every week. Of this form we are cleaning and maintaining to us healthy and healthful all along.

IS ONLY SO LONG

This book is a summary of several books, each book possibly has more than 200 pages and speak on the treated points more depth, nevertheless by my form to be pragmatic, like the direct things to the grain, without much roundup.

I have wanted to make a short book, pragmatical, easy to read for those people who have just a short time, in the shaken world of today.

With the reading and understanding of this book the things can work of direct form that they want to heal to obtain a total and happy life. It is possible to be worked the health, prosperity, love and much more. My idea is to be able to spread these techniques of simple form to help many people to heal its processes by own account, since no healer, guru or doctor can work your processes and learnings, really these people can guide you and only teach you, since everything is healed from inside. If you want to change your world, first you must change and its surroundings will change with you....a learned thing in the Law of the Attraction.

If for some reason the reader wants to go deep in the subjects, next I recommended some interesting books.

THANK YOU.....

BOOKS RECOMMENDED FOR ITS READING

The Healing code - Alex Loyd and Ben Jonson

The money and the Law of the Attraction -   Esther and Jerry Hicks

The Success Does not arrive by azar. Lair Riveiro

The Power is Within You - Louise Has.

The Law of the Attraction -   Esther and Jerry Hicks

Metamedicine - Claudia Rainville

Law of the attraction, myths and truths on the Secret - Dr. Camilo Cruz

Many Bodies, a same soul - Bryan Weiss

Reach Dad, Poor Dad - Robert Kiyosaki.

Magical words - Jocelyne Ramniceanu (Ho´ponopono)

Printed in Poland
by Amazon Fulfillment
Poland Sp. z o.o., Wrocław